I0538710

at *His* feet

La-Tricia Suber

ISBN: 979-8-9916585-8-4

Published by ICXII Publishing
9570 Regency Square Blvd, Jacksonville, FL 32225 USA
Copyright © 2025 La-Tricia Suber. All Rights Reserved

DAY 1 – THE POWER OF REPENTANCE:

Turning Back with Your Whole Heart

Key Scripture: *"Repent, then, and turn to God, so that your sins may be wiped out, that times of refreshing may come from the Lord."* — Acts 3:19

Theme: Repentance is not about shame—it's about returning. It doesn't push you away from God. It pulls you back to Him.

Where have I been holding on to things God is asking me to release?

_____

_____

_____

_____

Is there anything I've been excusing that I now need to confess?

_____

_____

_____

_____

What would it look like to return to God with my whole heart—not just in behavior, but in desire?

_____

_____

_____

_____

Write a personal letter of repentance to God today. Be honest. Be raw. Let it be real. Then listen for His response.

_____

_____

_____

_____

_____

_____

_____

_____

_____

_____

_____

_____

_____

_____

_____

_____

_____

_____

_____

_____

_____

_____

_____

_____

_____

_____

_____

_____

_____

_____

DAY 2 – THE KEYS & THE VOICE

Hearing and Obeying God

Key Scripture: *My sheep listen to my voice; I know them, and they follow me." —John 10:27*

Theme: You can't use the keys of the Kingdom if you don't know the King's voice.

Where have I delayed obedience in my life?

_____

_____

_____

_____

What do you believe God is whispering in this season?

_____

_____

_____

What would radical obedience look like today?

_____

_____

_____

_____

Surrendering Through Fasting

Key Scripture: *"Even now," declares the Lord, "return to me with all your heart, with fasting and weeping and mourning... Rend your heart and not your garments. Return to the Lord your God, for He is gracious and compassionate..."* — Joel 2:12–13

Theme: Fasting is not about starving your body; it's about feeding your spirit.

Where have you grown cold or distant in your relationship with God?

_____

_____

_____

_____

Write a prayer of return and surrender to Him today.

_____

_____

_____

_____

DAY 4 – OBEDIENCE OVER SACRIFICE:

When Saying Yes Costs Something

Key Scripture: *"To obey is better than sacrifice, and to heed is better than the fat of rams."* — 1 Samuel 15:22

Theme: God values obedience over religious performance.

Is there anything God has asked of you that you've delayed or reasoned away?

_____

_____

_____

_____

What "sacrifices" have you offered to God that may have replaced true obedience?

_____

_____

_____

_____

Write a **fresh yes** to Him today—even if it's uncomfortable, inconvenient, or costly. *Ask: "God, where do You want my yes today?" Then listen—and write it down.*

_____

_____

_____

_____

DAY 5 – SPEAK, LORD:

Hearing the Whisper

Key Scripture: *"After the fire came a gentle whisper."* — 1 Kings 19:12

Theme: God often speaks in stillness, not in noise.

What distractions do I need to silence to hear God more clearly?

_____

_____

_____

Have I been waiting for a loud answer when God may be speaking softly?

_____

_____

_____

Write out a moment in your life when you felt God speak clearly—even if it wasn't dramatic. Then ask Him: *"What are You whispering to me now?"* And be still long enough to hear.

_____

_____

_____

_____

DAY 6- LIVING SACRIFICE:

Offering Yourself Daily

Key Scripture: *"Present your bodies as a living sacrifice, holy and pleasing to God—this is your true and proper worship."* — Romans 12:1

Theme: Fasting is presenting your life on God's altar again.

What area of your life feels the hardest to lay down right now?

_____

_____

_____

What would it look like to trust God with it?

_____

_____

_____

Write a prayer of surrender for that specific area today—be honest, even if it feels messy. Let it be your personal offering on the altar.

_____

_____

_____

_____

DAY 7 – REFINER'S FIRE:

Purifying for Purpose

Key Scripture: *"He will sit as a refiner and purifier of silver..."* — Malachi 3:3

Theme: Fasting exposes the impurities so God can refine them.

What has the fire revealed in me this week?

_____

_____

_____

Are there thoughts, behaviors, or patterns surfacing that God is asking me to release?

_____

_____

_____

Write a declaration of what you're believing God to purify and what you're trusting Him to build in its place.

_____

_____

_____

DAY 8 – CLING TO THE WORD:

Anchored in Truth

Key Scripture: "…Love the Lord your God, listen to His voice, and hold fast to Him. For the Lord is your life…" — **Deuteronomy 30:20**

Theme: God's Word anchors us when emotions can't.

What verse has sustained you in past hard seasons?

_____

_____

_____

_____

Where do you need God's Word to anchor you right now?

_____

_____

_____

_____

Find a verse that speaks to your current situation—write it down, speak it out loud, and carry it with you all day like a lifeline.

_____

_____

_____

_____

DAY 9

Breaking Generational Curses

Key Scripture: *"Christ redeemed us from the curse of the law by becoming a curse for us..."* — **Galatians 3:13**

Theme: What started before you can stop with you.

What generational patterns do you recognize in your family line—emotionally, spiritually, financially, or relationally?

_____

_____

_____

_____

Ask the Holy Spirit to show you anything you've unknowingly agreed with.
Then write a personal prayer declaring what you are breaking... and what you are building in its place.

_____

_____

_____

_____

_____

_____

_____

_____

_____

_____

_____

_____

DAY 10

My House Will Serve the Lord

Key Scripture: *"As for me and my house, we will serve the Lord."*
— Joshua 24:15

Theme: Take authority over your home's atmosphere.

What have you tolerated in your home that doesn't reflect the heart of God?

_____

_____

_____

What would it look like to create a space for peace, worship, and unity?

_____

_____

_____

Write a prayer or declaration of faith over your household. Name each room if needed. Bless it in your own words.

_____

_____

_____

_____

_____

_____

_____

_____

DAY 11 – YOUR NAME IS FAVOR:

Walking in Kingdom Identity

Key Scripture: *"Surely, Lord, You bless the righteous; You surround them with Your favor as with a shield."* — Psalm 5:12

Theme: When you walk with God, you are the open door.

Where have you been questioning your visibility, worth, or identity?

_____

_____

_____

What doors are you believing God to open—not through force, but through favor? Write a truth statement today about who you are in Christ. Read it out loud. Let it reshape how you walk

_____

_____

_____

_____

_____

_____

_____

_____

_____

_____

Breaking Mental Strongholds

Key Scripture: *"Be transformed by the renewing of your mind..."* — Romans 12:2

Theme: You don't just need a new situation—you need a new mindset.

What negative thought loops or internal narratives have you believed for too long?

_____

_____

_____

_____

What would God say in place of those lies?

_____

_____

_____

_____

Write down the lie—then write out the truth from God's Word that replaces it. Speak that truth over yourself daily.

_____

_____

_____

_____

DAY 13

Breaking Agreement with Rejection

Key Scripture: *"Be transformed by the renewing of your mind..."* — Romans 12:2

Theme: You don't just need a new situation—you need a new mindset.

What moments or relationships made you feel rejected, unwanted, or unseen?

_____

_____

_____

_____

What specific lie did rejection try to write into your identity?

_____

_____

_____

_____

Now ask God: "What is Your truth about me?" Write it out and declare it aloud.

_____

_____

_____

_____

DAY 14 – COVERING OUR CHILDREN:

Securing Their Destiny in Prayer

Key Scripture: *""All your children shall be taught by the Lord, and great shall be the peace of your children." — Isaiah 54:13*
Theme: Your children may be small, but their purpose is great. Cover them daily.

What is the Holy Spirit revealing about your child (or children) during this fast?

_____

_____

_____

_____

Are there areas you've been anxious about that God is inviting you to cover in prayer, not panic?

_____

_____

_____

Write a personalized prayer or prophetic declaration over your child's life. Include their name and specific promises from God's Word.

_____

_____

_____

_____

Interceding Daily for Your Children

Key Scripture: *"Job would make arrangements for them to be purified. Early in the morning he would sacrifice a burnt offering for each of them..."* — Job 1:5

Theme: Consistency in prayer is one of the greatest gifts you can give your children.

What has tried to pull you away from daily, intentional prayer for your children?

_____

_____

_____

Ask the Holy Spirit to show you what consistent intercession could look like in this season.

_____

_____

_____

Write one short but specific daily declaration you will speak over your child this week. Make it personal and faith- filled.

_____

_____

_____

_____

DAY 16 – STANDING IN THE GAP:

Interceding for Adult Children

Key Scripture: *"I will contend with those who contend with you, and your children I will save."* — Isaiah 49:25

Theme: They may be grown, but your prayers still go ahead of them.

Where have you felt fear, guilt, or helplessness regarding your grown child's life or choices?

_____

_____

_____

Write a prayer of surrender today. Release the need to control, fix, or chase. Now, write a declaration of who your adult child is becoming—**not based on what you see,** but based on what **God has promised.**

_____

_____

_____

_____

_____

_____

_____

_____

DAY 17 – ONE FLESH:

Fasting for Your Marriage

Key Scripture: *"What God has joined together, let no one separate."*
— Mark 10:9
Theme: Your marriage is not just emotional—it's spiritual.

What lie or fear has been silently shaping your attitude toward your marriage?

_____

_____

_____

What would it look like to believe God for restoration instead of settling for survival? Write a declaration of life over your marriage today. Include any dry areas and what you want to see God breathe into again.

_____

_____

_____

_____

_____

_____

_____

_____

_____

_____

_____

DAY 18 – LOVE THAT LASTS:

Grace for the Journey

Key Scripture: *"Love bears all things, believes all things, hopes all things, endures all things."* — 1 Corinthians 13:7

Theme: Love is more than a feeling—it's a spiritual choice.

Where have I let irritation or frustration creep into the way I speak, think, or respond in my relationship?

_____

_____

_____

What's one way I can show intentional love this week—without waiting for it to be returned? Now write a love note, a prayer, or even a text you *wish* you had the courage to send—start there. Let love grow again through intentionality.

_____

_____

_____

_____

_____

_____

_____

_____

_____

_____

_____

DAY 19 – VISION AND CLARITY:

Praying for Supernatural Direction

Key Scripture: *"Where there is no vision, the people perish..."* — Proverbs 29:18

Theme: God doesn't just give dreams—He gives the steps too.

What areas in your life feel foggy or uncertain right now?

_____

_____

_____

_____

Have you been asking God for answers—or for alignment with His voice?

_____

_____

_____

_____

Write a simple prayer asking God for clarity and confidence in your next step. If He's already shown you something—write it down again and thank Him.

_____

_____

_____

_____

_____

_____

_____

DAY 20 – BOLD OBEDIENCE

Moving Without All the Answers

Key Scripture: *"By faith Abraham, when called to go… obeyed and went, even though he did not know where he was going."* — Hebrews 11:8

Theme: You don't need all the steps—you just need the next one.

Where have I hesitated because of fear, uncertainty, or a need to see "the whole picture"?

_____

_____

_____

What is one next step God is asking you to take today—even if it's small? Write it down. Then, write a bold "yes" beside it as an act of surrender and obedience.

_____

_____

_____

_____

_____

_____

_____

DAY 21 – FORMATION OVER COMFORT:

Surrendering to the Process

Key Scripture: *"Let perseverance finish its work so that you may be mature and complete, not lacking anything."* — James 1:4

Theme: You're not being punished—you're being prepared.

Where have I been resisting the process God is using to grow me?

_____

_____

_____

_____

What does it look like to surrender again today—even in the discomfort?

_____

_____

_____

_____

Write a simple prayer or affirmation that says: *"I trust the Potter, even when I don't see the masterpiece yet."*

_____

_____

_____

_____

_____

_____

_____

DAY 22 – THE JOSEPH SEASON:

Hidden But Favored

Key Scripture: *"The Lord was with Joseph, and he was a successful man... in the house of his master the Egyptian."* — Genesis 39:2

Theme: The hidden place is not punishment—it's preparation.

Where in your life do you feel hidden, delayed, or passed over?

_____

_____

_____

_____

How might God be using this season to form something in you that success could never teach?

_____

_____

_____

_____

Write a letter to God from the hidden place. Be honest, then write a sentence of trust that declares: *"Even here, You are with me."*

_____

_____

_____

_____

_____

_____

_____

_____

DAY 23 – OPEN DOORS:

Walking Through with Courage

Key Scripture: *"See, I have placed before you an open door that no one can shut."* — Revelation 3:8

Theme: Favor isn't random—it's assigned.

Is there a door in front of you that you've been afraid to walk through?

_____

_____

_____

_____

What would it look like to trust God with action, not just prayer?

_____

_____

_____

_____

Write the door down. Then write your response:
"Yes, Lord—I'll walk through."

_____

_____

_____

_____

DAY 24 – FREEDOM FROM FEAR:

You're Not Going Back

Key Scripture: *"For God has not given us a spirit of fear, but of power and of love and of a sound mind."* — 2 Timothy 1:7

Theme: Fear is not your portion—faith is.

What fear has been whispering in the background of your mind lately?

_____

_____

_____

_____

What truth do you need to speak louder than that lie?

_____

_____

_____

_____

Write a **faith declaration** that replaces the fear—something short, powerful, and true. Speak it every time fear tries to creep back in.

_____

_____

_____

_____

DAY 25 – WARFARE & WORSHIP:

Winning the Unseen Battle

Key Scripture: *"As they began to sing and praise, the Lord set ambushes against the men... and they were defeated."* — 2 Chronicles 20:21–22

Theme: Worship isn't filler—it's a weapon.

What battles have you been trying to fight in your own strength?

_____

_____

_____

How can you begin to praise in advance today, even before you see the breakthrough?

_____

_____

_____

Write out a prayer of worship—not asking for anything, just declaring who God is. Then take a few minutes to sit in that posture of praise.

_____

_____

_____

_____

DAY 26 – FAITH IN THE FIRE:

Standing in the Testing

Key Scripture: *"Even if He does not… we will not serve your gods or worship the image of gold."* — Daniel 3:18

Theme: Even if He doesn't… I'll still trust Him.

What is your **"even if"** declaration today? *(Even if God doesn't heal… Even if it doesn't change yet… Even if I have to wait…)*

_____

_____

_____

_____

How do you sense God is strengthening your faith in the fire rather than removing you from it?

_____

_____

_____

_____

Write it as a letter to God. Be honest but choose to anchor your trust in who He is—not just in what He does.

_____

_____

_____

_____

_____

_____

_____

_____

DAY 27 – PURPOSED FOR HOLINESS:

Living Set Apart

Key Scripture: *"Be holy, because I am holy."* — 1 Peter 1:16
Theme: Holiness isn't religious—it's powerful.

What area of your life is God gently highlighting for deeper holiness or surrender?

_____

_____

_____

_____

What does "living set apart" look like for you in this season?

_____

_____

_____

_____

Write a prayer of surrender for that area. Invite the Holy Spirit to help you walk it out with joy—not obligation.

_____

_____

_____

_____

_____

_____

_____

_____

DAY 28 – FRUIT OVER FAME:

Cultivating Christlike Character

Key Scripture: *"But the fruit of the Spirit is love, joy, peace, patience, kindness, goodness, faithfulness, gentleness and self-control..."* — Galatians 5:22–23

Theme: Character is greater than charisma.

Which fruit of the Spirit is God highlighting for you today?

_____

_____

_____

Where have you been prioritizing performance over inner transformation?

_____

_____

_____

Ask the Holy Spirit to show you how to cultivate fruit in both quiet moments and everyday decisions.

_____

_____

_____

DAY 29 – DIVINE STRATEGY:

Heaven's Blueprint for Earthly Work

Key Scripture: *"I am the Lord your God, who teaches you what is best for you, who directs you in the way you should go."* — Isaiah 48:17

Theme: You don't need a trend—you need a word.

What vision or dream have I been trying to figure out in my own strength?

_____

_____

_____

What pressure do I need to release so I can hear God's instructions clearly?

_____

_____

_____

Write down what you believe God is saying about the next step, not the full plan. Ask Him for peace before motion.

_____

_____

_____

_____

_____

_____

_____

DAY 30 – KINGDOM BUSINESS:

Inviting God Into Your Work

Key Scripture: *"But remember the Lord your God, for it is He who gives you the ability to produce wealth."* — Deuteronomy 8:18

Theme: Your business isn't just for provision—it's for purpose.

Where do you need God's wisdom, creativity, or peace in your work or business right now?

_____

_____

_____

_____

What fear, pressure, or "old way" of doing things do you need to surrender?

_____

_____

_____

_____

Write a prayer or declaration that realigns your work with Kingdom purpose—not just productivity.

_____

_____

_____

_____

DAY 31 – FILLED WITH POWER:

Finishing in Victory

Key Scripture: *"Jesus returned to Galilee in the power of the Spirit…"* — Luke 4:14

Theme: You're not leaving this fast empty—you're leaving filled.

What has God formed, revealed, healed, or broken in you during this fast?

_____

_____

_____

_____

Write your **personal post-fast declaration.** What will you carry forward from here? How has God equipped you?

_____

_____

_____

_____

_____

_____

_____

_____

_____

_____

_____

_____

_____

FOCUS FAST:

Forgiveness

DAY 1

The Weight I Can't Carry Anymore

Key Scripture: *"Come to me, all who are weary and burdened, and I will give you rest." — Matthew 11:28 (NIV)*

What is the specific weight I've been carrying?

_____

_____

_____

_____

How has holding on to this pain affected my peace or identity?

_____

_____

_____

_____

What do I need to hear from God today about this pain?

_____

_____

_____

_____

The Lie That Took Root

Key Scripture: *"You intended to harm me, but God intended it for good..." — Genesis 50:20 (NIV)*

What lie(s) have I believed because of this offense?

_____

_____

_____

_____

Where has that lie shaped my view of God, others, or myself?

_____

_____

_____

_____

What does God say instead? Write His truth as a replacement.

_____

_____

_____

_____

DAY 3

Forgiveness Is for Me

Key Scripture: *"Bear with each other and forgive one another... Forgive as the Lord forgave you."* — *Colossians 3:13 (NIV)*

Journal Prompt

What did God reveal to me during these 3 days?

_____

_____

_____

_____

What has shifted in my heart or my perspective?

_____

_____

_____

_____

Write a "release letter" to the person you're forgiving. (You don't have to send it —this is for you.)
Finish this sentence: "Now that I've forgiven, I can finally..."

_____

_____

_____

_____

_____

_____

_____

FOCUS FAST:

Forgiveness
from Betrayal

WHEN THE ONE WHO HURT
YOU WASN'T SUPPOSED TO

This Shouldn't Have Happened

Key Scripture: *"Even my close friend, someone I trusted, one who shared my bread, has turned against me." — Psalm 41:9 (NIV)*

Journal Prompt

Who hurt you—and how did it impact your trust, your identity, or your peace?

_____
_____
_____

_____

What have you been trying to carry alone?

_____
_____
_____

_____

What would it look like to begin releasing this to God?

_____
_____
_____

_____

Healing While Still Hurting

Key Scripture: *"The Lord is close to the brokenhearted and saves those who are crushed in spirit." — Psalm 34:18 (NIV)*

Journal Prompt

Where does the pain still feel fresh?

_____
_____
_____
_____

What would healing "look like" to you in this area?

_____
_____
_____
_____

What is God whispering to your heart in the middle of this process?

_____
_____
_____
_____

I Forgive So I Can Be Free

Key Scripture: *"It is for freedom that Christ has set us free. Stand firm, then, and do not let yourselves be burdened again by a yoke of slavery." — Galatians 5:1 (NIV)*

Journal Prompts

What does freedom look like for me now that I've chosen to forgive?

_____

_____

_____

_____

How can I continue this walk of healing after this fast ends?

_____

_____

_____

_____

What new declarations can I speak over my life instead of pain?

_____

_____

_____

_____

DAY 4

New Heart, New Love

Key Scripture: *"I will give you a new heart and put a new spirit in you..."* — *Ezekiel 36:26 (NIV)*

Where has my heart grown hard or guarded in this relationship?

_____

_____

_____

_____

What does loving with a "new heart" look like in this season?

_____

_____

_____

_____

What's one way I can show love today—even if I don't feel it yet?

_____

_____

_____

_____

DAY 5

Fighting the Right Enemy

Key Scripture: *"For our struggle is not against flesh and blood, but… against spiritual forces..." — Ephesians 6:12 (NIV)*

Where have I confused my spouse for my enemy?

_____
_____
_____
_____

What lie about our marriage needs to be confronted in prayer today?

_____
_____
_____
_____

How can I lead with love and humility in our next disagreement?

_____
_____
_____
_____

FOCUS FAST:

Restoring Communication

DAY 1

Fast Theme:
Rebuilding Bridges, Not Walls

Opening Scripture:
"Let your conversation be always full of grace, seasoned with salt..." — Colossians 4:6 (NIV)

Where have our words or tone been hurtful?

_____

_____

_____

Where have I avoided communication out of fear, pride, or fatigue?

_____

_____

_____

What does healthy communication look like to me—and what is one step I can take today?

_____

_____

_____

_____

DAY 2: SPEAKING FROM THE HEART

Creating Space for Truth

Key Scripture:

"Instead, speaking the truth in love, we will grow to become in every respect the mature body of Him who is the head—that is, Christ." — *Ephesians 4:15 (NIV)*

What fear has kept me from saying what I really feel?

_____

_____

_____

_____

Where can I create more emotional safety in our conversations?

_____

_____

_____

_____

What would I say if I knew I'd be received with compassion?

_____

_____

_____

_____

Learning to Listen Like Jesus

Key Scripture:

"Everyone should be quick to listen, slow to speak, and slow to become angry." — James 1:19 (NIV)

Where do I tend to shut down or get defensive when my spouse is talking?

_____

_____

_____

What would it feel like to listen without needing to fix or prove anything?

_____

_____

_____

_____

What can I ask today that invites my spouse to open up safely?

_____

_____

_____

FOCUS FAST:

Rebuilding Trust

DAY 1

Fast Theme:
Healing What Was Broken Without Hardening What Remains

Opening Scripture:
"Love always protects, always trusts, always hopes, always perseveres."
— 1 Corinthians 13:7 (NIV)

Where did trust first begin to break down?

_____

_____

_____

What has helped rebuild it in the past (if anything)?

_____

_____

_____

What do I need to release to God in order to take the next step?

_____

_____

_____

_____

DAY 2

Consistency Heals What Apologies Can't

Key Scripture:
"Whoever walks in integrity walks securely…"
— Proverbs 10:9 (NIV)

Where has inconsistency damaged trust in our relationship?

_____

_____

_____

_____

What small habits could help restore what words alone haven't?

_____

_____

_____

_____

DAY 3

Trusting Again Without Losing Yourself

Key Scripture:
"Above all else, guard your heart, for everything you do flows from it." — Proverbs 4:23 (NIV)

What beliefs do I need to release about trust and vulnerability?

_____

_____

_____

_____

How can I speak honestly without fear in this season?

_____

_____

_____

_____

FOCUS FAST:

Emotional Intimacy

DAY 1

Theme:
From Surface-Level to Soul-Deep

Opening Scripture:
"They were both naked, the man and his wife, and were not ashamed."
— Genesis 2:25 (NKJV)

Where have I pulled away emotionally in this relationship? Why?

_____

_____

_____

What would it feel like to be fully known—and still accepted?

_____

_____

_____

What's one honest conversation I've been avoiding but need to have?

_____

_____

_____

_____

When the Hearts Drift But Love Remains

Key Scripture:
"Draw near to God, and He will draw near to you." — James 4:8

What has caused us to drift emotionally?

_____

_____

_____

_____

What do I miss most about the closeness we once had?

_____

_____

_____

_____

_____

_____

_____

_____

DAY 3: SAFE TO BE SEEN

Cultivating Vulnerability

Key Scripture:

"Carry each other's burdens, and in this way you will fulfill the law of Christ." — Galatians 6:2

What would I say if I knew I'd be heard with love?

_____

_____

_____

_____

How can I create more emotional safety in our relationship?

_____

_____

_____

_____

_____

_____

_____

_____

FOCUS FAST:

DAY 1

Tearing Down Idols

Opening Scripture:
Exodus 20:3-4 (NIV)
"You shall have no other gods before Me. You shall not make for yourself an image in the form of anything… You shall not bow down to them or worship them."

What do I instinctively run to for comfort or validation before I run to God?

_____

_____

_____

_____

What has taken up more of my energy, attention, or affection than it should?

_____

_____

_____

_____

What would it look like to lay that thing down—not just for the fast, but for good?

_____

_____

_____

_____

What has God been gently asking me to surrender, and what am I afraid will happen if I do?

_____

_____

_____

_____

DAY 2

Who's Really Lord?

Key Scripture:
Matthew 6:24
Theme:
You can't serve two masters—and only One can save you.

What have you allowed to have more say in your life than God?

_____

_____

_____

What does it practically look like for Jesus to be Lord of your time, your relationships, your money, and your emotions?

_____

_____

_____

Where is God asking you to *reclaim the throne* of your life?

_____

_____

_____

_____

DAY 3

A Heart That's Whole Again

Key Scripture:
Psalm 86:11
Theme:
You were never made for divided loyalty.

Where have I been half-in with God?

_____
_____
_____
_____

What area of my life still feels split between faith and fear?

_____
_____
_____
_____

What would it look like to give God all of me again?

_____
_____
_____
_____

FOCUS FAST:

Financial Breakthrough

DAY 1

Theme:
God doesn't just give money—He gives vision, wisdom, and trust.

Opening Scripture:
"But remember the Lord your God, for it is he who gives you the ability to produce wealth..."— Deuteronomy 8:18 (NIV)

Where do I need to trust God more in my finances?

_____

_____

_____

Have I made money or comfort into an idol?

_____

_____

_____

What has God put in my hands already that I can use?

_____

_____

_____

Is He asking me to give during this fast—even if it's small?

_____

_____

_____

DAY 2

The Gift That Opens Doors: Sowing in Faith

Key Scripture:
Luke 6:38
Theme:
God uses your giving to unlock supernatural provision.

Where is God nudging me to sow—not just financially, but spiritually?

_____
_____
_____
_____

Write down a story or moment where giving led to unexpected provision.

_____
_____
_____
_____

DAY 3

The Blueprint for Wealth: Obedience & Stewardship

Key Scripture:
Deuteronomy 8:18
Theme:
God doesn't just bless—He teaches.

Where is God calling me to tighten my stewardship or step out in a financial assignment?

_____

_____

_____

_____

What new ideas, plans, or habits might be part of my breakthrough?

_____

_____

_____

_____

CLOSING CHAPTER

The final words to seal this 31-day journey.

Final Reflection:

What God Has Done in Me

USE THIS SPACE TO REFLECT ON WHAT SHIFTED DURING THIS FAST:

What did God reveal to me about myself?

_____

_____

_____

_____

What area of my life feels lighter?

_____

_____

_____

_____

What idols or burdens have I laid down?

_____

_____

_____

_____

How have I heard God more clearly?

_____

_____

_____

_____

What truth has replaced a lie I was carrying?

_____

_____

_____

_____

What new habits or rhythms do I want to carry forward?

_____

_____

_____

_____

What idols or burdens have I laid down?

_____

_____

_____

_____

How have I heard God more clearly?

_____

_____

_____

_____

www.ingramcontent.com/pod-product-compliance
Lightning Source LLC
Chambersburg PA
CBHW051554120626
46551CB00013B/1515